the
heart
of
awareness

selections from
    Jean Klein
    H.W.L. Poonja
    Nisargadatta
    Ramana Maharshi
    Huang Po
    Swami Ahedananda

compiled by
peter ingle

Copyright © 2013–2017 Peter Ingle

the heart of awareness

All rights reserved

ISBN 978-0-9746349-8-2
ISBN-13: 9780974634982 (Peter Ingle)

No part of this publication may be reproduced, stored, or transmitted in any form or by any means electronic, mechanical, photocopying, recording, or otherwise, without written permission from the author.

Published in the United States of America
Library of Congress Cataloging-in-Publication Data

Ingle, Peter M.
the heart of awareness

The selections in this book come from six masters who recognized that behind all observable phenomena in ourselves and in the world there resides a pure, silent, motionless, unperturbed awareness.

This truth has been taught under different names for millennia, but these masters reduce it to its core: that the essence of enlightenment is pure awareness being aware of being aware.

the heart of awareness

Selections from *I AM* 1

Selections from *Wake Up and Roar* 37

Selections from *I AM THAT* 67

Selections from *Be As You Are* 83

Selections from *Zen Teaching of Huang Po* ... 91

Selections from *Philosophy of Work* 111

the heart of awareness

This book would not have been possible without the generous permission of the publishers.

Thank you

Jean Klein
(1912–1998)

Selections from
I AM

Edited and compiled by Emma Edwards
© 2006 & 2007 Non-duality Press

LIBERATION does not concern the person. Liberation is freedom from the person.

The idea of being a person, an ego, is nothing other than an image held together by memory.

The mind will lead you astray until you perceive its true nature.

Your attention is constantly turned either toward objects or to ideas. You know yourself only in relation to something. A sense of being, without qualification, is completely unknown to you.

We discover ourselves in attention. This attention transcends the experience and the experiencer. It is pure awareness. The waking state and dream state are imposed upon this still awareness.

When you have once glimpsed your real nature, it solicits you. There is nothing to do, only to be attuned to it.

It is not the mind which attunes to awareness, but awareness which absorbs the mind.

Once the mind is free from activity, fear, and dissatisfaction, you will see that your only true desire is to be.

The Self is searching for itself. A deep understanding of this brings us spontaneously back to our home ground.

When you are free from the mental habits of activity and passivity, you will find yourself in your natural quiet attention; that in which thoughts appear and disappear. Whether thoughts come to mind or not, you will not be bound to them.

When you are active or passive regarding the coming and going of feelings and thoughts, you see and act from the ego-center. But when you come to know the illusory nature of this center, you are automatically out of the process.

When you are in awareness, there's no more center. Awareness is aware of its surroundings and aware of being aware.

The ultimate non-state is awareness itself. Thoughts and pulsations appear in this awareness.

Don't try to witness. Realize that you are the witness and that you cannot try to be it. It is enough that you become fully aware that you are the witness.

You are not the doer of your acts. You are the awareness from which action stems.

Uncover the person who feels something is missing. The moment you no longer believe you are the body and the mind, the energy used in this error will be freed. Leave the mind and body free to be what they are and you will no longer be their slave.

Once the mind stops trying to grasp, it returns to a state of equilibrium where everything points toward silent awareness.

This quiet mind is not the absence of thought.

What you are is the light behind all perceptions.

Awareness can never become an object. It is neither outside nor inside. It is free from time and space. It is the vastness, the container, in which all states and objects appear.

If consciousness could be perceived, it would not be our totality.

The meditator can never find peace, god, or happiness because it (the meditator) belongs to the mind, to the intellect.

The total emptiness which you experience during meditation is, in a way, still an object. Emphasize the knower of the empty mind and not the empty mind itself.

Once you are knowingly this awareness, you no longer identify with the mind.

We are accustomed to being attentive towards some-thing, but pure attention is not focused on an object. It is free from any memory. It is simply expanded alertness.

The question "who am I" will be found to have no answer. You can only formulate and explain that which you are not. What you fundamentally and continually are cannot be put into words or reasoned about.

What you fundamentally are is always here, always complete. It needs no purification. It never changes.

You cannot discover or become truth, for you are it. There is nothing to do to bring it closer. See only that you are constantly trying to go away from what you are.

Silent awareness is not a state, but is the continuum in which all states, all things, appear and disappear.

You are the witness, the onlooker, standing on the bank watching the river flow on. You do not move. You are changeless.

Silent awareness is beyond the absence or presence of thoughts, words, activity, or passivity. Nothing whatsoever can affect this tranquility.

Sooner or later you will find there is no room for personal identity. There remains only a deep inner peace from conflict and problems.

You know your thoughts, your emotions and feelings. But you don't know the knower.

Everyday life appears in consciousness. You are this consciousness but are not what appears day after day.

We have taken it for granted and believe ourselves to be this 'me'. The 'me' always seems to be at the center of things. It is a false appropriation.

You are seeking your real nature. What you are looking for is what you are, not what you will become. Looking for something to become is completely conceptual, on the level of ideas.

The body and mind have no reality in themselves. They are entirely dependent on consciousness. They change constantly. It is the changeless background that allows us to realize this.

We take ourselves for something that we are not. All our actions and thoughts, our ideas of success and failure, real and unreal, come out of this false idea of being.

The perceiver is distinct from what is perceived. The person, the individual, the ego is but an object of perception. It is only by our habit and error that we identify ourselves with our perceptions.

Suffering and pain are strong pointers inviting us to inquire just who is suffering. The accent shifts from the perceived to the ultimate perceiver whose nature is joy beyond pleasure or its absence.

Thought arises from silence and loses itself in silence. Its function is to point towards that from which it arises—the ultimate, which is unthinkable.

The ego is nothing but a thought amongst many others. It is a product of memory, of the past.

You exist because you are an expression of pure consciousness. Your nature is to be alert and aware of what appears in you, but you must be knowingly aware, must know yourself to be aware.

Our true nature is not, properly speaking, a state. It is the very substance, the background to all states. It is silent presence.

All effort to eliminate or become is useless because the attempt is itself part of what you are trying to eliminate.

The direct way is so simple. You abide in the seeing and the rest takes care of itself.

Searching for yourself in any way is a complete waste of time. This must become a perfectly obvious fact to you.

All this accumulation of states and sensations and techniques is nothing but vanity. It still belongs to the person who looks for security and confirmation.

Conflict and problems all derive from the mind as it tries to justify its existence. When you see this suddenly, in the utter conviction of total awareness, you become conscious of what you have never ceased to be.

The true aim of our existence is to be, without conditioning.

If the mind remains confused and keeps striving to attain something, however subtle, however open-minded, it will inevitably finish up by turning round and round in circles within the same old structures.

The ego likes to direct things and circumstances according to its wishes.

The ego has its origins in a mental image: "I am the body."

We do not know things. We only know them in appearance, which is nothing but name and form. To know a thing itself, we must go far beyond its appearance.

As what you are is not a state, it is a waste of time and energy chasing more and more experiences in the hope of coming closer to the non-experience.

In an experience you see that there is still an experiencer who is stuck in the pattern of going in and out of states. Global understanding is the sudden awareness that the perceiver of these states is unaffected by them; that they appear *in* the perceiver.

Awareness is the essential element.

Any action influenced by the concept of the individual 'I' traps us in a vicious circle. In these circumstances we are the doer, the thinker, and are chained in a psycho-logical relationship to the act or thought.

In truly creative moments, everything takes place without an 'I' interfering.

Everything points toward awareness and is re-integrated in it. When once we take the object as a pointer to what we are, a path opens up before us.

We can never find enlightenment in the realm of thoughts and concepts. All striving by the 'me' is a hindrance.

The Self is silent awareness, but this silence is beyond concept and cannot be defined in terms of silence as opposed to noise. Thus, trying to rid ourselves of agitation so as to attain a state of silence keeps us in conflict. If, on the contrary, we accept the agitation as an expression of silence, it dissolves in the acceptance.

You cannot hope to rid yourself of agitation if you remain on its wavelength. You must listen to it as a whole. It then dies into silence, for it is nothing but silence.

The Self is unthinkable, beyond mind and the psyche.

All striving to objectify the knower which cannot be conceived of in terms of concepts prevents us from directly perceiving our true nature.

The world always appears to us according to the point of view we adapt. For the senses it is form, for the mind it is ideas, for the Self it is consciousness.

The light is always there before the object appears.

Whatever you do you are always consciousness. It cannot be otherwise. Confusion invades you once you believe yourself to be the doer, the thinker, the willer. In reality you are purely the witness of your actions.

Memory is only a thought amongst many others. When we clearly recognize memory as being only a thought, the illusion of time leaves us.

Thought, memory, and time arise from still awareness.

We often try to master the mind, to quiet it through concentration, but soon realize that concentration and distraction belong equally to the divided mind. We cannot possibly master the mind by means of the mind.

Awareness is beyond dispersion and concentration.

Our true Self is never to be found in a perception, in an object.

Consciousness is the hearth from which sparks fly and lose themselves. We erroneously identify with these sparks. They are but fragments.

All perceptions are objects perceived in consciousness. Fear is therefore an object, a perception.

Taking oneself to be a person is a habit. It is a desire to be distinct from one's surroundings, different from others.

The perceived leads directly to perceiving. It is the shortest way to consciousness.

You cannot perceive the perceiving because you are it.

The truth seeker emphasizes the seeing. He does not explore the object as such, but uses it only to establish himself in the seeing.

An artist is looking for something, and when he finds it he keeps it. The truth seeker finds himself only in the looking.

We should absolutely take note how all our thoughts and doings come out of a center and involve choice.

Awareness without tension—where you are involved and do not seek a conclusion—is total awareness. All intention to manipulate the future comes from a partial point of view, that of the ego.

Culture, education, social, and economic factors have conditioned our body and mind. Our true being is neither implicated in nor influenced by these limits. It is completely free.

Awareness is not in a state. States are in awareness. It is only awareness which makes states possible.

Because we do not know ourselves except in relation to objects, we always strive to find ourselves in relation to objects.

With the deep understanding that the doer, the willer, is an illusion, you will find yourself in complete stillness following an act or thought.

If you feel tired, really look at it and you will spontaneously find yourself uninvolved in it. Do the same with all the worries that preoccupy you.

It gradually dawns on us that we are not the person, that we are this awareness. This becomes more and more tangible.

When we really wake up, what we previously called being awake seems also like a dream.

Only in the complete absence of yourself is there total presence.

Stillness does not mean a peaceful mind. The mind can be temporarily calm, but this is not stillness.

It is in the nature of the mind to move. Stillness is not in the slightest way affected by this movement.

Everything is an expression of silence.

It is the object, the body-mind, which suffers.
What we are is the knower of the suffering.

An ambitious mind can never be a free mind.

Whatever we do or think, we are awareness.

If awareness were only a mental function like
all others, it would disappear like all functions.
But it never disappears.

The mind exists within awareness. Its very nature is to express this awareness by means of name and form.

Thoughts, feelings, and actions appear in succession before the witness, leaving their imprint in your brain. Recalling them makes you believe in a continuity which is actually nonexistent.

Above all, do not try to be a witness. This would only be a projection and would keep you in the frame of ideas and expectations.

The mind is simply an activity which comes and goes. The witness records this lack of continuity.

You live in awareness, which is sacred. This is your true nature. In this non-state there is neither desire nor anxiety.

It is inherent that the human condition try to locate itself somewhere, in a bodily sensation or a thought. If we let things flow freely, we will discover ourselves to be observation.

You are not the body, neither the healthy nor the unhealthy body.

When we know that we can never find what we are seeking in an object, no matter how subtle, then our attention shifts to observation itself.

The Self is always aware. It is we who are asleep. We are awake in objects but not in the Self.

When you are attentive to something, you are fixed on the object. But when you are simply in attention you are free from all grasping.

Timeless presence, the background behind and between perceptions and thoughts, is pure consciousness.

It is through the known that the unknown expresses itself.

The ultimate expresses itself in space and time and dies back in itself.

It is only the mind that asks questions.

True joy is not linked to outside circumstances. It flows directly from the Self.

The ultimate end—if there is one—is to free yourself from this identification with the person.

You can find yourself free from thought, but you can never cease being what you are fundamentally.

You must leave behind the idea of improving. There is nothing to be found, nothing to achieve. Searching and wanting to achieve something are the fuel for the entity you believe yourself to be. Be simply aware of the facts of your existence without wanting change.

No effort can lead you to this ultimate harmony. Every attempt leads you farther away.

The strongest insight is an instantaneous apperception that your total being is always present, always in the now.

The unknown is the closest to us; too near to be perceived.

Ultimate desire is living without desire, where there is no longer any room for the idea of being somebody.

Everything you take to be personal, everything the 'I' creates or respects, is false. Liberation consists in being free from the 'me'. Understanding this is a sudden opening to a new dimension.

Problems, weariness, boredom, depression stem only from the mistaken notion of taking ourselves for a certain person, with certain ideas, a particular background, and so on.

Our difficulties come when our projections into the future in the hope of attaining some result are thwarted.

Only when we live in our wholeness, free from the person, free from all goals, preferences, and choice, can there be a full expression of life.

If we observe things more closely, we soon come to realize that it is the body that is doing the acting and the mind the thinking.

Consciousness is its own light. It does not need a vehicle. Objects, on the contrary, depend entirely on consciousness. They could not be perceived otherwise.

In letting go of all trying, time no longer exists. There is no more expectation.

We are taught to superimpose the past on the present and future, and so we lose the excitement, the newness, of the moment.

While the child still focuses on the object of inquiry, the mature seeker focuses on the inquiring itself, and one day discovers himself to be the inquiring.

In awareness there is no thought of action or not. You simply function in the moment itself.

The last and the first obstacle is the idea of being somebody.

In the practical approach there is no disciple and no teacher. If there were, there would only be teaching on a mental level.

All that the mind can know is not you.

You are neither this nor that. You are the knower of all.

H.W.L. Poonja
(1910–1997)

Selections from
Wake Up and Roar
Satsang with H.W.L. Poonja
Volumes 1 and 2

© 1992 Pacific Center Publishing

YOU HAVE TO DO nothing to be who you are. You are always here. You deny it. You deny your greatness.

There is the fear of embracing this emptiness. You don't see anything there. No name. No form. Unknown. Absolutely empty. You need courage to hug that emptiness of no name and no form.

Nobody can help you. Help can only take you to the edge.

When you look from there, from emptiness, you see everything. Nothing beyond that. Nothing to do. Only to be as you are.

Emptiness is your own nature. This is what you are, and really you need not do anything about it.

When you don't give rise to a thought, you return to emptiness.

We have a conception that by practice we shall become free. We become enlightened in this instant only, not as a result of ten years' practice.

You don't need memory. Memory is ego. Neither the mind nor the ego exist. They are just your own desires. Yet in reality they don't exist.

When you decide to kill the ego, this is the ego itself.

One is always free and one is always alone.

Emptiness is not heavy.

The mind has to abide on an object. Allow the mind to abide nowhere and what will be the result?

The awareness of consciousness does not change. States may change. And you are that awareness.

To become something, to expect something, you have to do something. To remain "I am" you don't have to do anything. Its fullness is emptiness.

Empty everything from the pockets of your mind. Search where there is no distance and nothing to do. It is too easy for you.

You can't lose emptiness.

Sit quietly and do not move your mind or intellect. Then observe the observer. This is your true nature from where everything else comes.

If you make any effort or use any method of trying to achieve something at some distant future, this will bring you into time. And time is mind. So this will be the play of mind only. But your original nature is empty.

We cling to the body, the mind, the senses, for safety. We don't realize that by letting go of these things we have true peace.

The observer has to observe something. What you observe is through the mind. So whatever is gained through the observation is only mental. Who is the observer? Tackle the observer.

The body has no capacity to be enlightened.

Nobody teaches this emptiness. Everyone wants to run an ashram or commune. When you speak of emptiness there is nothing more to learn.

Doing can never get you to that which you already are. Doing is moving away from that, not toward it.

After enlightenment the momentum of your desires may continue, but they do not touch the Self.

There is no time at all. Time is only ignorance. Millions and billions of years is an instant.

As long as there is change there must be something changeless to watch the changes. Wherever there is change there must be a substratum of changelessness. That is your own nature. On this, body, mind, and all phenomena are projected.

A real teacher will not give you anything to do. No method. Nor can he give you freedom. You have to face yourself—a very pleasing situation.

To be as you are now at this very instant, what means are needed?

When you become the seer, you see the illusion and then it does not exist.

Emptiness is always alone, unchanging. It is now. Now itself is empty.

You can avoid the slaughterhouse if you want to. Otherwise you will be taken by the butcher, the king of death.

You have to surrender to that supreme unknown emptiness and function from there.

You quiet the mind by looking at it. Look at it and it will be quiet. Then it will be objectified. Some subject must be there to look at this object. Then you are separate from what you are looking at.

You can count on your fingers the number of people who truly want to be free.

You must recognize your own nature or you will not be happy.

No name. No form. That is your nature. Will you recognize it? Will you discharge into it?

Keep quiet and become quietness itself.

You don't need any method, any practice, and concept, any book. Any doing will take you away from it, not toward it.

All the appearances are not true. They were not there before the beginning and they will not be there after the end.

If you touch that point of who you are, you are fullness itself. What can you desire? Desires don't exist.

Don't cling even to the emptiness. Take off even from the emptiness itself.

This journey will take you back to your home. It will not push you to any new kind of dimension. You cannot become or get what you are not. You have to be what you already are.

Don't hold onto the present either. The concept of the present must also be transcended. Transcend name and form. Transcend the light also.

When you are yourself, there is no fear. You are aloneness. Time doesn't touch you, mind doesn't touch you, fear doesn't touch you. They are all concepts. You are beyond all that.

This instant of time is beyond the concept of time. This is your home, your final abode where nothing appears. This is the knowledge of the unknown which is empty. Nothing is there. No wants, no needs, no desire. This is peace. This is your own self. You don't have to attain it, achieve it, or acquire it by any method whatsoever. No effort is needed to reach there.

When you have true peace, you will desire to see if there is even deeper peace. It is an unending search in the direction of the unknowable. This activity is the direction of inactivity. It is activity within inactivity. This joy is your nature. It is not searching for something else.

You must go alone. No one can do it for you. All beaten tracks are the past.

The ultimate truth is that there is no teacher, no teaching, and no student.

Just be quiet. Sit absolutely quiet. No thought. In quietness, in silence, the Self arises by itself.

Anything you desire to achieve is a limitation.

Who reaches the Self except the Self? The fundamental obstacle to realization is precisely the notion that this realization is still awaited.

Guard carefully against supposing that silence has anything to do with either thinking about it or not thinking about it.

The Self cannot be reduced to anything capable of being said, thought, or taught—or to the negation or absence of thought.

It is you, in your own depths, who is the supreme peace and joy.

Mantras, prayers, and ritual are excellent up to a certain point. But the time comes when all that has to be left aside. You have to take a leap into the beyond.

Stay quiet. Wherever the mind goes, bring it back to its source.

When you use the word 'I', refer to total emptiness.

Find out how to get rid of the identification with that which changes. Identify with that which does not change.

Awareness without subject or object must be dis-covered. This is your own awareness.

'I' arises and behaves as if it is awareness. All trouble arises from this.

When you search for 'I' it disappears, leaving pure awareness.

It cannot be done by doing anything, reading anything, or practicing anything. It does not depend on any mind or any body. It shines by its own light.

Look behind the 'I'. Look underneath the 'I'. Look for the source of 'I'.

The question is: what is this no-I from where everything rises?

Beyond name and form, which are not real, who are you? What's left? That is what you are. It is not graspable by the sense or the mind. It is untouched and unspoken. It cannot be defined.

No religion teaches you to just keep quiet. Very few people spend five minutes in their house keeping quiet.

Your mind projects a manifestation and then runs after the projection. Instead of running out with the senses, arrest the mind and direct it to its source.

To see a light you don't need a light. It is the light itself. It reveals itself by itself.

Consciousness is the basis, the foundation, the source.

True meditation is concentration on the awareness itself: being aware of this awareness. Keep aware and awareness will reveal the truth of itself. Awareness meditating on itself is meditation.

Consciousness cannot be understood, perceived, or conceived. It has no observer. Consciousness is consciousness alone.

Keep digging into un-arisen thought and see what happens. Keep going farther in. Don't give rise to any thought, and discover who you are.

Break off all relations with the mind itself. Then you are left alone. Stay by yourself and find out.

If all the known is rejected, in front of you is the unknown. You become unknown and merge into the unknown, because they are identical.

Be a representative of truth.

Simply stay quiet. Something else is going to take charge of you. You simply watch what happens and you keep quiet. Just keep quiet and let something arise from within—that peace you have never seen. keep quiet for some time and it will reveal itself.

What is waking up? Establishment firmly into the Self, by the Self, with the Self, for the Self.

The Self is untouched. Absolutely untouched.

Direct your mind to the source and do not think. That is the prescription for wisdom.

You always have a light within you, but you don't turn toward it. Instead you see this light shining on outer objects.

Your attention is reflected on objects and this reflection attracts you to objects. Instead, find out where this beauty, this luster, this reflection is coming from. It shines by its own light. You only have to turn toward it.

Look within the Self, by the Self. All the rest is with the body and mind, and all results will be mental or physical.

You are sitting in emptiness and you think you are the owner because of the walls of the house you are sitting in. You are still in the emptiness.

Thought is ego.

From where is the 'I' arising? Plunge there. Dive deep into the unknown.

You impose the notion of activity (I am doing this, I will do that) on the substratum of inactivity. There is something inactive that doesn't work at all. From there arises the notion of activity and you get involved in activity. If you then attach to certain things, you are lost. If you know where this actually arises from—that it arises from non-action, from the non-activity—you will realize freedom.

Nothing happens in awareness.

Find out who the seer is.

The highest state is no-state. When there is no mind, there is no state. Your true nature is no-state. Remove all concepts and this will be your own state whether you are walking, talking, eating, or sleeping.

When the breeze pays a visit to the fish market, the garden, or the cemetery, does it accept or reject anything? This stateless state is something like that.

You are on the stage. This drama is given to you. if you know you are the source, you can play any role and not be tainted.

Introduce yourself to your Self and there is no need for remembering who you are.

The quickest method, the most direct method, is inquiry into the source of "I am."

Aren't you aware of whatever you are doing? This awareness is your Self.

If you are conscious of consciousness within the consciousness, there is no problem, whatever you do. Nobody knows this, and so they suffer.

With all practices, mind is involved. Inquiry is striking the root of the mind itself.

When you know who you are, death can't touch you.

Expectation is garbage. Expecting to become something else at a later date is a basket of garbage on your head.

When there is no there and no here and no where, this is consciousness itself from where everything arises and falls.

Consciousness alone is, and nothing ever exists beyond this consciousness. Once having known it you become one with consciousness.

Your part of the job is to go to the beyond. And then it will take charge. It will conduct every routine of your life.

Hell is the mind turned outward and saying, "I am the body." The mind turned inward is heaven. And how to win the kingdom of heaven? Surrender to awareness.

Everyone is searching outside through the senses. Whatever you see, wherever you see name and form, it is not true. This is the decision and the discernment.

Why not spend the rest of your life engaged in this affair?

No monastery has been successful at producing enlightenment. Running away from life has never paid anyone.

All kinds of training are still being done because it is easier to do them than to sit quietly.

The mind doesn't like to be quiet. The mind likes to engage in activities and exercises. When you are not active mentally, this is peace.

After enlightenment there is no ego and no doership. You will abide in something else.

When you recognize yourself—as when a river discharges into the ocean and is no longer a river—all qualities are gone.

When you are free, freedom takes charge of you.

Sit quietly and keep quiet. This quietness is your nature. It will bring you home.

Nisargadatta
(1897–1981)

Selections from
I AM THAT
Talks with Sri Nisargadatta Maharaj

Translated by Maurice Frydman, and edited by
Sudhakar S. Dikshit. Published by The Acorn Press,
Durham, NC. 2nd rev. ed., 2012. Selections text
copyright Chetana Pvt. Ltd., Mumbai, India.

YOU ARE AWARE—you need not try to be. What you need is to be aware of being aware. You are always conscious of the mind, but you are not aware of yourself as being conscious. The mind must learn that behind the moving mind there is the background of awareness which does not change. Awareness is unattached and unshaken. It is lucid, silent, peaceful, alert, and unafraid; without desire and fear.

The man who carries a parcel is anxious not to lose it. He is parcel-conscious. The man who cherishes the feeling 'I am' is self-conscious. The sage holds onto nothing and cannot be said to be conscious and yet he is not unconscious. He is the very heart of awareness.

From awareness of the unreal to awareness of your real nature there is a chasm which you will easily cross once you have mastered the art of pure awareness.

Ultimately you come to something so simple that there are no words to express it.

The Self stands beyond the mind, aware but unconcerned. You are the Self. Leave the mind alone. Stand aware and unconcerned and you will realize that to stand alert but detached, watching events come and go, is an aspect of your real nature.

You imagine that you do not know yourself because you cannot describe your Self. But whatever can be described cannot be your Self, and what you are cannot be described. To know that you are neither in the body nor in the mind, though aware of both, is already self-knowledge.

The pure witness watches what is going on and remains unaffected. In pure awareness, nothing ever happens.

When I look at myself through the mind, I see numberless people. When I look beyond the mind, I see the witness. Beyond the witness there is the infinite intensity of emptiness and silence.

The witness is merely a point in awareness. It has no name and form. It is like the reflection of the sun in a drop of dew. The drop of dew has name and form, but the little point of light is caused by the sun.

Through the film of destiny your own light depicts pictures on the screen. You are the viewer, the light, the picture, and the screen. Even the film of destiny is self-selected and self-imposed.

Consciousness is always of something. Awareness is total, changeless, calm, and silent. Awareness makes consciousness possible.

When you know what is going on in your mind, you call it consciousness. Then comes awareness: the direct in-sight into the whole of consciousness; the totality of the mind.

Awareness is the cognizance of consciousness as a whole.

Step back from the action to consciousness. Leave action to the body and mind. It is their domain. Remain as pure witness, till even witnessing dissolves in the supreme. When the body is no more, the person disappears completely without return. Only the witness remains, and the great unknown.

Realize that all happens in consciousness and that you are the root, the source, the foundation of conscious-ness. What you are conscious of is neither you nor yours. Yours is the power of perception, not what you perceive.

Give all your attention to the question, "what is it that makes me conscious?"

Space and time are the body and the mind of the universal existence. But at the root of the universe there is pure awareness, beyond space and time, here and now. Presence in the now is a state ever at hand but rarely noticed. Once you are well established in the now, you have nowhere else to go.

Wherever you go, the sense of here and now you carry with you all the time. It means you are independent of space and time; that space and time are in you, not you in them.

The mind should be normally in abeyance. Incessant activity is a morbid state. Just leave your mind alone.

Watch your thoughts and watch yourself watching your thoughts. The state of freedom from all thoughts will happen suddenly, and by the bliss of it you shall recognize it.

Awareness is the point at which the mind reaches out beyond itself into reality.

Whenever a thought or emotion or desire or fear comes to your mind, just turn away from it. I am not talking of suppression. Just refuse attention. It has nothing to do with effort. Just turn away. Look between the thoughts rather than at the thoughts. When you happen to walk in a crowd, you do not fight with every person you meet. You just find your way between.

It is all quite simple. Turn away from your desires and fears and from the thoughts they create, and you are at once in your natural state. Leave your mind alone. That is all. Don't go along with it. Thoughts dominate you only because you are interested in them.

Silence is one. It is always there, at the back of words. But the mind craves for formulations and definitions, always eager to squeeze reality into a verbal shape. Reality is essentially alone, but the mind will not leave it alone.

Keep quiet. Do your work in the world, but inwardly keep quiet. Then all will come to you. Your hope lies in keeping silent in your mind and quiet in your heart. Realized people are very quiet.

All that happens happens in and to the mind only, not to the source of 'I am'. Once you realize that all happens by itself, you remain as witness only, understanding and enjoying, but not perturbed. Remain as the silent witness only.

In the mirror of your mind all kinds of pictures appear and disappear. Knowing that they are entirely your own creations, watch them silently come and go. Be alert, but not perturbed. You see the picture, but you are not the picture.

Pay no attention to your desires and fears. Let them come and go. Don't give them the nourishment of interest and attention.

To be what you are you must go beyond the mind, into your own being. It is immaterial what is the mind that you leave behind. Understand your own mind and its hold on you will snap.

Relax and watch the 'I am'. Reality is just behind it. Keep quiet, keep silent. It will emerge. Or rather, it will take you in.

Moods are in the mind and do not matter. Go within. Go beyond. Cease being fascinated by the content of your consciousness. When you reach the deep layers of your true being you will find that the mind's surface play affects you very little.

There is a vastness beyond the farthest reaches of the mind.

The very idea "I am self-realized" is a mistake. There is no 'I am' in awareness.

The idea 'I am free' is as false as the idea 'I am in bondage'. Find out the 'I am' common to both and go beyond.

Liberation is never of the person. It is always from the person. The person is but a shell imprisoning you. You are not a person. Find who you are.

The person is of little use. It is deeply involved in its own affairs and is completely ignorant of its true being. The person may be conscious, but is not aware of being conscious. It is completely identified with what it thinks and feels and experiences.

Freedom means letting go. People just do not care to let go everything. They do not know that the finite is the price of the infinite, as death is the price of immortality. Spiritual maturity lies in the readiness to let go everything. But the real giving up is in realizing that there is nothing to give up, for nothing is your own.

Understand first that you are not the person you believe yourself to be. What you think yourself to be is mere suggestion of imagination. There is nobody who 'does'. All happens, including the idea of being a doer.

The dissolution of personality is followed always by a sense of great relief, as if a heavy burden has fallen off. The personality gives place to the witness. Then the witness goes and pure awareness remains. The person merges into the witness, the witness into awareness, awareness into pure being.

When you happen to desire or fear, it is not the desire of fear that are wrong and must go, but the person who desires and fears. The person should be carefully exam-ined and its falseness seen. Then its power over you will end.

Go beyond the 'I am the body' idea and you will find that space and time are in you, not you in space and time. Once you understand this, the main obstacle to realization is removed.

The body is born and dies. While alive it attracts attention and fascinates so completely that rarely does one perceive one's real nature. It is like seeing the surface of the ocean and completely forgetting the immensity beneath.

It is the person you imagine yourself to be that suffers, not you. Dissolve it in awareness. It is merely a bundle of memories and habits.

Ramana Maharshi
(1879–1950)

Selections from
Be As You Are
The Teachings of
Sri Ramana Maharshi

Edited by David Godman
Arkana Penguin Books © 1985 Sri Ramanasraman

YOU ARE AWARENESS. Awareness is another name for you. Since you are awareness, there is no need to attain or cultivate it.

At one stage you will laugh at yourself for trying to discover the Self which is so self-evident.

The real is as it is always. We are not creating anything new or achieving something which we did not have before.

The mind does not exist without the Self. The Self exists without the mind. The wrong knowledge of "I am the body" is the cause of all the mischief.

The Self is a state of simple awareness. The Self is prior to consciousness. No one can ever be away from the Self.

Bliss is not added to your nature. It is merely revealed as your true natural state. Nothing more can be predicated of the Self than that it exists.

You, being the Self, want to know how to attain the Self. It is like a man being at a place asking how many ways there are to reach that place and which is the best way for him.

The Self alone exists. When you try to trace the ego, which is the basis of the perception of the world and everything else, you find the ego does not exist at all, and neither does all this creation that you see.

Thought is projected out from the Self. Find out from where it rises. Thoughts will cease to rise and Self alone will remain.

If we look on the Self as the ego, then we become the ego; if as the mind, we become the mind; if as the body, we become the body.

Take no notice of the ego and its activities, but see only the light behind. The state free from thoughts is the only real state.

It is the mind that veils our happiness.

Abiding in the Self, one need not worry about the mind.

The idea of time is only in your mind. There is no time for the Self. Time arises as an idea after the ego arises. But you are the Self beyond time and space. You exist even in the absence of time and space.

Time and space are in you. All that you see around you is in you.

A guru will not give you anything you have not already got. It is impossible for anyone to get what he has not got already.

We are always the Self, only we do not realize it.

The ordinary man lives in the brain unaware of himself.

The Self is the substratum of all that is seen.

The seeker ultimately reaches the Self and there finds unity as the prevailing note.

The world neither exists by itself, not is it conscious of its existence.

The Self is god. For if god be apart from the Self, he must be a self-less god, which is absurd.

You now think that you are an individual, that there is the universe, and that god is beyond the cosmos. So there is the idea of separateness. This idea must go. For god is not separate from you or the cosmos.

Knowing the Self, god is known. In fact, god is none other than the Self.

God the creator, the personal god, is the last of the unreal forms to go.

the heart of awareness

Huang Po
(died 850 A.D.)

Selections from
Zen Teaching of Huang Po
*The Teachings of
Sri Ramana Maharshi*

Translated by John Blofeld
Grove Press, NY © 1958 John Blofeld

TO MAKE USE of your mind to think conceptually is to leave the substance and attach yourself to form.

Awake to the One Mind and there is nothing whatsoever to be attained. This is the real Buddha.

If you do not awake to this Mind substance, you will overlay Mind with conceptual thought. You will seek the Buddha outside yourself, and you will remain attached to forms, pious practices, and so on, all of which are harmful and not at all the way to supreme knowledge.

The substance of the Absolute is inwardly motionless, and outwardly like a void in that it is without bounds or obstructions. It is neither subjective not objective, has no specific location, is formless, and cannot vanish.

This Mind is no mind of conceptual thought, and it is completely different from form.

If you can only rid yourself of conceptual thought, you will have accomplished everything.

Let there be a silent understanding and no more. Away with all thinking and explaining.

Even if you go through all the stages of progress towards Buddhahood, one by one, when at last, in a single flash, you attain to the full realization, you will only be realizing the Buddha-nature which has been with you all the time; and by all the foregoing stages you will have added to it nothing at all. You will come to look upon these eons of work and achievement as no better than unreal actions performed in a dream.

The people of the world, blinded by their own sight, hearing, feeling, and knowing, do not perceive the spiritual brilliance of the source-substance.

The Self is not an activity.

To awaken suddenly to the fact that your own Mind is the Buddha, that there is nothing to be attained, or a single action to be performed—this is the supreme way.

Learn only how to avoid seeking for and attaching yourself to anything. Where nothing is sought, this implies Mind unborn. Where no attachment exists, this implies Mind not destroyed. And that which is neither born nor destroyed is the Buddha.

Men are afraid to forget their minds, fearing to fall through the Void with nothing to stay their fall. They do not know that the Void is really void.

This spiritually enlightening nature cannot be looked for or sought, comprehended by wisdom or knowledge, explained in words, contacted materially, or reached by meritorious achievement.

Attach yourself to nothing beyond the pure Buddha-Nature which is the original source of all things.

Every single thing is just the One Mind. When you have perceived this you will have mounted the Chariot of the Buddhas.

The Real Mind cannot be exactly described, but when you have a tacit understanding of its substance, it is there.

Just let your mind become void and environmental things will void themselves. Let principles cease to stir and events will cease stirring of themselves.

The wise eschew thought.

All the concepts you have formed in the past must be discarded and replaced by void.

Put all mental activity to rest and thus achieve tranquility. Beginningless time and the present moment are the same.

Let each thought go as though it were nothing, or as though it were a piece of rotten wood, a stone, of the cold ashes of a dead fire. Just make whatever slight response is suited to each occasion.

Mind is like the sun: forever in the void, shining spontaneously.

What is called supreme, perfect wisdom implies that there is really nothing whatever to be attained.

Mind resembles a void. Seek for naught but this, else your search must end in sorrow.

Whatever the senses apprehend resembles an illusion, including everything ranging from mental concepts to living things.

All the Buddha's teachings just had this single object—to carry us beyond the stage of thought.

The moment of realizing the unity of Mind and the Substance which constitutes reality may truly be said to baffle description.

it is because you do not know your real Mind that you delude yourself.

Mind knows no divisions into separate entities. Mind is above all activities.

Whatever has form is illusory.

The Great Void is perfection wherein is neither lack nor superfluity; a uniform quiescence in which all activity is stilled.

Remain uniformly quiescent and above all activity. Do not deceive yourself with conceptual thinking, and do not look anywhere for the truth. All that is needed is to refrain from allowing concepts to arise.

In truth, not a single thing exists which can be attained. You awaken to the intrinsic voidness of phenomena.

Full understanding can come to you only through an inexpressible mystery. The approach to it is called the gateway of the stillness beyond all activity. A sudden comprehension comes when the mind has been purged of all clutter of conceptual and discriminating thought activity.

Your consciousness *is* the Buddha.

Whence does your consciousness arise?

You may talk the whole day through, yet what has been said?

Every single one of the myriads of phenomena in the universe is the Buddha (Absolute). This substance may be likened to a quantity of quicksilver which, being scattered in all directions, everywhere reforms into perfect wholes. When undispersed it is one piece: the one comprising the whole and the whole comprising the one.

Prevent your mind from going on travels outside itself.

The three worlds will vanish if you can reach the state beyond thought.

If you were to remain quiescent and to refrain from the smallest mental activity, the Substance of Mind would be seen as a void—you would find it formless, occupying no point in space and falling neither into the category of existence or non-existence. Know this and rest tranquilly in nothingness.

If you would learn how to achieve a state of non-intellection, immediately the chain of causation would snap.

Renounce the error of intellectual or conceptual thought processes, and your nature will exhibit its pristine purity.

Even the most strenuous of your efforts is doomed to fail. Indulging in such practices implies your failure to understand the real meaning of Mind.

Your true nature is something never lost to you even in moments of delusion, nor is it gained at the moment of enlightenment.

Ah, it is a jewel beyond all price.

Your sole concern should be, as thought succeeds thought, to avoid clinging to any of them. Nor may you entertain the least ambition to be a Buddha here and now.

To gaze upon a drop of water is to behold the nature of all the waters in the universe.

In contemplating the totality of phenomena, you are contemplating the totality of Mind.

The phenomenal universe and Nirvana, activity and motionless placidity—all are of the one Substance.

In this world, how few are they who have lost their egos.

The perceived cannot perceive.

The fundamental nature of all phenomena is close beside you, but you do not see even that.

Avoid pondering things in your mind.

Ah, could you but restrain each single thought from arising.

With the merest desire to attach yourself to this or that, a mental symbol is soon formed. So let your symbolic conception be that of a void, for then the wordless teaching of Zen will make itself apparent to you.

There is absolutely nothing which can be attained. The belief that enlightenment can be attained belongs to the doctrine of those sects which do not understand the truth.

One who comprehends the truth of "nothing to be attained" is already seated in the sanctuary where he will gain his enlightenment.

Only when your mind ceases dwelling upon anything whatsoever will you come to an understanding of the true way of Zen.

The way of the Buddhas flourishes in a mind utterly freed from conceptual thought processes.

The primordial darkness is the sphere in which every Buddha achieves enlightenment.

The world is full of vexations arising from the transitory phenomena around us.

My advice is to give up all indulgence in conceptual thought and intellectual processes. When such things no longer trouble you, you will unfailingly reach supreme enlightenment.

Do not permit the events of your daily life to bind you, but never withdraw yourself from them.

Never allow yourself to mistake outward appearance for reality. Avoid the error of thinking in terms of past, present, and future.

Do not permit the least movement of your mind to disturb you.

Be diligent. Be diligent.

Swami Abhedananda
(1866–1939)

Selections from
Philosophy of Work

Vedanta Society, NY © 1902 Swami Abhedananda

THERE IS WITHIN us something that transcends all activity which is unchanging, immovable, and eternally at rest—that which, in the midst of our varied activities of mind and body, remains always inactive.

From the minutest atom up to the grossest material form there is constant motion. Nowhere is there rest. One thing, however, moves not. One thing is at rest.

The reader knows that he is sitting and also that he is reading. He distinguishes two distinct objects of know-ledge. But the consciousness with which he perceives them remains the same.

The knower of all the experiences of your childhood is just the same as the one who knows what we are doing now. The knower is unchangeable and not bound by the conditions which govern the changeable.

Anything which takes form in the mind and is conditioned by time and space must change. But the knower, not being a condition of mind or limited by time and space, does not change.

If we analyze our mental activities and study the nature of the knower, we find that it is the permanent source or intelligence above the mind and beyond thought; that it is in reality neither thinker nor actor.

When the knower comes to be identified with the conditions of the mind, of the organs of work, and of the body, we appear to be doers and seek the results of our work.

The goal is to learn this lesson of disassociating the knower from all changes of body and mind, and never confounding our mental and physical conditions with the immutable being within us.

The moment that we think that our body is a part of the universal body, our mind not separate from the common mind, and that our souls, being part of one universal soul are most intimately connected with one another, all activity assumes a new meaning for us.

The true nature of the knower is above all activity.

Nothing in the universe can ever exist without depending upon the existence of the universal knower which manifests through each individual form.

We are in reality the knower, the Atman. Anything else is not permanently connected with us.

Not realizing that we transcend all activity, we have imagined ourselves one with our mental modifications and our organic functions; and having fettered ourselves with desires, we are struggling to satisfy them. When, however, we recognize that these desires are not permanently related to the true Self, that they exist in mind only, and that we can use them as a means of attaining perfect freedom, then they will cease to bind us and we shall find rest and peace in the midst of our troubles.

It is when we forget that we are the knower, and become identified with anger, passion, or hatred, that we fall under their dominion.

The true Self is the unattached, witness-like knower of all things who remains unchangeable in the midst of changes of mind and body.

The soul is not created from nature, but nature is working for the experience of each individual soul.

If we study our own souls carefully, we find that our mind, intellect, senses, and body are within the realm of phenomena, while the real Self is something which stands as a witness outside and beyond mind, intellect, body, and senses. That witness-like something within us is beyond nature and its laws. It is already free.

The work done by mind and body is in reality not performed by the true Self, but by nature.

The real Self never suffers. It is already divine and free from birth and death. When we know this, life becomes worth living here and now. Otherwise we may perform duties forever without finding peace and happiness.

Other books by Peter Ingle
(also available on Kindle and iBooks)

OUR FATHER
Talks About
the Inner Meaning of The Lord's Prayer with
Temerlen P. Gillis

The Little Book of Awareness

Inside the Mind of Awareness

The Little Book of
Transforming Negative Emotions

Think Before You Write

www.ingramcontent.com/pod-product-compliance
Lightning Source LLC
Chambersburg PA
CBHW020657300426
44112CB00007B/413